Text Copyright © 2020 by Brittani Grant
Illustrations for this book were rendered digitally.

All rights reserved.
ISBN: 978-1-7354379-0-3

Published in the United States by
Dawson Mama Publishing, LLC a Dawson Inspired
Company, Decatur, Georgia.

THE HOLY BIBLE, NEW INTERNATIONAL VERSION®
NIV® Copyright © 1973, 1978, 1984 by
International Bible Society. ® Used by permission.
All Rights Reserved worldwide.

For more information about this title or author:
Email: SBNPublishing@yahoo.com

The content of this book is not intended to be a substitute for professional medical advice, diagnosis, or treatment, and does not constitute medical or other professional advice. The author nor the publisher is offering or advising its content as replicable.

SPECIAL THANKS

This book is dedicated to God who has given me the vision to write this based on my own understanding. The late Minister Shelia D. Hayes, my mother, who has taught me to be the woman that I am, and to know God. May her soul rest in paradise. She was a special saint, full of God-given wisdom and knowledge. I will forever miss you and follow in your footsteps.

To my dad, C.H.R, and my other mom, Mrs. G. They have always kept it real, and never cared about our feelings more than our well-being. Thanks for keeping it real.

My best friend, MG, through thick and thin has always supported me, and encouraged me through this entire process. May we always stay friends and grow old together.

I cannot forget my dear brother "B," who at times felt the need to preach to me, when I did not want to hear it. A "Mr. Know it All," however, he knows more than most and is always there when needed. Good or bad, we have stuck together in whatever life has brought us. We have been through a lot together. I have always told people that he is, "My Heart."

A special thanks to my Noont Nookie, "Hot Mess Ri," my daughter. She often gives me the strength to carry on by allowing God to use her, in many ways. I am blessed to have such a daughter who God has already given words of wisdom. Her smile is priceless and her heart is so pure! She has helped me get through many rough days.

    Finally, to the remainder of my family and friends, you know who you are. You have supported me in the simplest ways, and you are all appreciated.

From Dreams to Purpose
By
Brittani Grant

Contents

Introduction — 1

Communicating with God — 5

Battle of the Sexes — 8

Please Stop the Violence — 12

Each Man for Himself — 15

Why Can't We All Just Get Along — 18

Worth a Million Smiles — 21

Little Sunshine — 23

An Answered Prayer — 25

Steps to Interpreting Your Dreams — *Included*

Introduction

We as humans may often ask ourselves, *"What is our purpose in life here on this earth?"* Some of us find the answers early in our lives. Others go years seeking fulfillment to be whole and to make a difference in someone else's life. Some may fail to find what makes them special.

Everyone does not have the gift to be a doctor, lawyer, or have a great profession in which they can impact a person's life. However, everyone has a purpose to make a difference in this world somehow.

I have asked myself, "What am I destined to be, or perhaps, who?" I have a theory that there must be a reason why I am still living, with all the different times I have faced danger in my life. I should have been dead many times.

My whole life has been a testimony and now I am here to find my purpose. The goal of this book is to give myself, as well as others the understanding we need in order to make our lives worth living.

First, we must know that there is a *being* that is much greater than ourselves. We must then get to know that *being*. Next, we must know ourselves. Finally, we must know what we are seeking to find.

The Bible says to ask, and it shall be given unto you,

seek and you shall find, knock and the door shall be opened.

If we believe that there is a *being* greater than oneself, we must know that somehow that being, I have learned to know so well on a personal level, must also have a place to live.

I believe in God. I call him my heavenly father. He lives in a place called Heaven. He sits high and he looks low. He is the creator of heaven and earth.

Through my beliefs, understanding, and life experiences with God; I have found that there is more to my life.

Have you ever wondered how and why things happen the way they do? Well, everyone has their own theories. I can only speak from what I know to be true, based on what I have experienced. My theory tells me that not only is there a heaven and earth, but there is also a hell.

I believe that God also lives in the spiritual world. He lives within us. We are man, spirit, and soul. This brings me to my main point. Everything in the entire universe connects with each other. This means that we have a connection with God.

Some of us may not know or understand how, but we are about to find out. As stated earlier, God is my heavenly father, according to my beliefs. Whenever I need to speak to Him, I go to Him through prayer.

Prayer is a form of communication with God. You may ask yourself, "How do I hear back from Him once I have spoken. The answer is quite simple. He can speak through prophecies, visions, premonitions, and/or dreams.

A **prophecy** is the foretelling or prediction of what is to come. Something that is declared by a prophet (a person who speaks for God). It can also be known as a divinely inspired utterance or revelation. To be a prophet means to speak as a mediator between God and humankind.

A **vision** is the act or power of sensing with the eyes. The act or power of anticipating that which will or may come to be is defined as a prophetic vision.

A **premonition** is a feeling of anticipation of or anxiety over a future event. It can be a forewarning.

A **dream** is a succession of images, thoughts, or emotions passing through the mind during sleep. A dream analysis is the analysis of dreams as a means of gaining access to the unconscious mind.

The mentioned terms will help give us some understanding through our quest.

There must be some form of communication between God and the seeker. Now that we have found out some of the many forms of communication, we must find out which way God communicates back with us and how to interpret the messages that he sends.

I have done my research and found some of those answers to help find my purpose. The rest lies within.

1
Communicating with God

When you look back at the questions that were asked earlier, what did you come up with? It is much deeper than you think. God works with us and through us. During your everyday life when you have had a thought about anything, where do you think that thought came from?

What about when we are about to walk into a large building and have a gut feeling that something just doesn't feel right? Why is it that we may feel that way? We must look deeper than that.

How about when we feel we may have had a Deja vu moment? Could it have been a vision or premonition instead, trying to warn us from making a mistake?

Something must be in the universe that is trying to get our attention and communicate. Unless we are able to tap into our inner gifts and find out how to use them, it all remains just a thought.

My beliefs tell me that God wants to communicate with us, as much as we do with him. Please know that he is not the only being that wants to communicate. The evil Satan who lives in a place called Hell, also tries to communicate with us to get us to do bad things.

We have to know when God is trying to speak with us versus other entities that are here to harm us. Having that said, we can now get a better understanding of what is really going on. God does not communicate with everyone in the same way. Some people, he gives a vision of what is to come or a premonition of what to watch out for.

He may also speak to us in a small still voice. According to Matthew 22:14 in the Bible, "Many are called, but few are chosen." With that being said, we all can hear his voice whether we pay attention or not, but only a few of us are called to carry certain tasks. For example, everyone is not chosen to pastor a church, but we all are called to minister or speak to others in whatever way the spirit leads us.

The most common form of communication from God are in our dreams. It all starts in our sleep or place of rest. Some people have dreams that are to give them a sign or guidance. Other people have dreams that actually manifest itself into the natural world. I believe that during our times of rest, God feels that it is the perfect time to communicate with us because we are not distracted with our busy worldly lives.

Scientist have come up with the theory that when we are

asleep we go through six stages of sleep. One in which we dream, and they call that the "REM stage" or "Rapid Eye Movement." What does this mean? REM came about when scientist established when a person is asleep their eyes move back and forth. It appears to look as though that person is watching a movie.

Our dreams were said to tell a story. How do we fall asleep and wake up? We definitely do not wake up by ourselves or from the alarm clock if that is what you think. God allows us to wake up and fall asleep every day and night. Knowing this tells me that the dreams that we have during sleep are for a reason.

Not only does God want us to rest, he also wants to relay a message through our dreams. How do we know what our dreams mean? It is called interpretation. Once we have a dream, we must write it down upon awaking and pull out the keywords and feelings that stand out to us the most. Then we must compare them with instances that have occurred in our waking life.

It is possible that you may not remember all of your dreams but you should still record whatever you may remember, if anything at all. This I believe will give us the answer to our prayers, help us understand our purpose, and what we must do next in order to succeed with greatness.

2
Battle of the Sexes

There were a group of three, two men and a woman. I was the woman in the group. We found ourselves running from what we thought to be our enemies. It was almost like we were running for our lives. There were two other groups who we considered to be our enemies, and we had to flee from them. One of the groups included all men, and the other all women.

The group of men were evil, however, surprisingly, all the women were not. Two of the women out of three were good people. They just happened to be misled by the wrong person, the evil sister.

My group was quite different from the rest of them. We all had supernatural powers and could fly. Better yet, we were half human mixed with a little bit of Wolverine and Spiderman.

We had sharp claws that shot out our fingers when we went into protection mode. Despite the fact that we were different in many ways, no one knew so because we dressed and acted normal as everyone else, we blended in.

The first part of this dream took place inside of a parking garage at one of our local malls. I found myself running alone from the three evil men until my friends came to rescue me.

We were flying, hiding, and jumping everywhere. At first, I could not recall what these evil doers wanted from us, but it had to have been over something that would make them want to kill us.

What was the motive to their madness? Oh, now I remember. It was to rule the world. The next thing you know, we ended up inside of a hotel where there were long ropes of beautiful orange beads hanging down from the elevator. The elevator sat in the middle of the building. Throughout the whole battle, we fought while swinging from the ropes and jumping from window to window.

Once that terror ended, I met a new person. He was a homeless, African American, and a homosexual. He had a good heart. He had no name, so I will just call him John Doe. This special individual had supernatural powers as well. He had no knowledge of his powers.

I took him in and cleaned him up. I trimmed his hair and put him on a nice suit. When I got through with him, he looked like Keenen Wayans in the movie, "A Low-Down Dirty Shame." Towards the end of the movie, before Shame got ready to save his friend Peaches from the mob, he cleaned himself up and got suited up. He was sharp! John Doe looked the same, sharp. John then became a part of our group.

At one instance, he saw a couple of men doing bad things that he did not agree with. He followed them to a hotel. The men went up to their room with a woman and began having sex with each other. John sneaked into the room by climbing up a wall, kicking in the window from the living room of the suite, and entering the dark bedroom. The police got a noise complaint from one of the neighbors and kicked in the door of the hotel room.

John fled the scene, and my mind went fast-forward to the third scene. Here comes the group with the three sisters. One of them had a six-year-old son. He had no idea that his mother or aunts had supernatural powers, nor did he know that he had an evil aunt.

The small family went to a strange building and stepped out, leaving the boy in the car. The three evil men from the first scene found the boy and tried to kidnap him. The mother had a gut feeling that her son may have been in danger, so the sisters ran back to the car to save him. Suddenly, the evil men disappeared, and the only people left was John, the three sisters, and I.

The dream ended with John and I, going to a club where we ran into the sisters again. Two of the sisters asked us to join them but not the evil sister. She had so much envy in her. She shouted, "No" and left! We left soon afterwards, and that was the end of the battle of the sexes.

Interpretation:

In this dream God was giving me a message of what he was about to do in me, as well as reminding me that I am never alone. In the beginning of the dream, I mentioned swinging from an orange rope. During my research I found that orange is symbolic of endurance and strength. It is the color of a fire flame and the symbol of the sun. Orange represents the red of passion and the yellow of wisdom.

God also gave the message of transformation, a new me, as I had transformed John in the dream. He also forewarned me that I should not follow the wrong crowds. He will send me who I need, and he has done just that.

3
Please Stop the Violence

    This dream occurred on Riverdale Road in College Park, Georgia. It was early one morning when my co-worker and I went to get breakfast. I felt someone watching me. It felt more like this person was spying on me, but I ignored it. Later that night when it was time for us to get off of work, my coworker left and I had to lock up alone.

    As I was walking to my car I noticed that my mother's ex-husband Jerry was walking in the parking lot. I called his name and he walked over to speak. It was cold outside, so I asked him to get inside of my car so that we could talk. Jerry got in from the backseat, and we talked for a while. Soon afterwards, a Caucasian man came from out of nowhere. It just so happened that Jerry knew this man.

    He walked up to the side of the car where Jerry was sitting and demanded that he let down the window. They began talking and making smart remarks at each other. Jerry got angry and started using profanity. The man did not like that, so he shot Jerry several times. Jerry died and the man fled.

I screamed in fear and took off running. The man saw me and came to kidnap me. I had to walk around town with him all night being his slave. He held his gun towards me the entire time. He demanded I go into different businesses to get food and other things for him.

I finally got away by playing reverse psychology on him and quoting multiple bible verses. I told him that God sees all, and he will be punished for what he has done.

The next day at work we moved to a new location down the street from the old office. My coworker told me that the man had been there looking for me. I was frightened, so I told her that if anyone called or stopped by looking for me, tell them that I was no longer there. I put out a search warrant for a Caucasian murderer and kidnapper. The police found and arrested him. I then had to go down to the police station to identify him.

When I got there, he was the third person lined up behind the glass. I lied and said that I did not see him there. Why would I do such a thing? In my mind, I wanted God to personally deal with this evil man, in which he did. Later, this man really suffered. He had learned his lesson, and he found me so that he could make amends for what he had done.

He took a friend and I to the beach and spent a lot of

money on us. Was I crazy or what? I wondered what happened between him and Jerry the day he shot him.

Could it have been drug related? I never asked because I did not want to jeopardize being hurt, knowing what this man was capable of doing.

Interpretation:

Some dreams can also come from the last thought before going to sleep. I had just spoken to my cousin. She was telling me that her husband was out working late, and she was home alone with her daughter.

She saw a strange man walking outside of her window, and stated that the man walked around for a while, then left. The next day she went to buy a gun. "God has not given us the spirit of fear but of power, love, and a sound mind" -- 2 Timothy 1:7. *He will always protect us.*

4
Each Man for Himself

Here I am deciding to go back to school. I had gone to college in Georgia and Tennessee, but this time I wanted to try something different, so I enrolled for school in Florida. My sister-in-law, Bianca was from Florida, so we took a trip down in December. We went to an ice rink, and we were sliding across the ice, riding on a sled. Later, Bianca went home and I stayed for school.

I was upset because at the colleges that I previously attended I was a Junior, however, Florida put me back in High School because they were missing classes on my transcript. I then joined what I thought was their football team but later found out it was ROTC.

During our training one day, we all headed to a large field. The field had a large hole in it. It appeared to look as though a meteor had hit. We had to lay down on our backs in the middle of the hole, holding on to the grass to stop from sliding down. We were then assigned to wear a different color glittered team shirt.

Every so often, a small portion of the team would climb

out of the hole and start to walk back to the school, which we called our base. The commander called each team by color to take turns leaving one at a time. The team that I was a part of had finally been called to leave, but we got caught in danger on our way back.

We had to run in zigzags from whatever was after us. I was extremely scared, but I kept running and never looked back.

Suddenly out of nowhere a huge bird swooped down and grabbed one of the boys from our team with his feet and flew off into thin air. I want to say that the bird was a vulture. I had no idea what the vulture did with the boy. Maybe it had eaten him.

The vulture returned, but not as a bird. It came back as former Atlanta Falcons player, Mike Vick. He walked us back to the hole. Vick preached about how we should not be afraid to return to base, so we returned to base.

This time everyone as a whole left instead of splitting up into groups. We thought that everything would be okay this time, but we were mistaken. The running began again. I somehow ended up running down into the woods alone, where I saw a monster.

Interpretation:

In the dream I was upset about being sent back to high school. This led me to understand that some things you cannot control so the best thing to do is read the Serenity prayer. I do what I can and leave the rest to God.

"God grant me the Serenity to accept the things I cannot change, courage to change the things I can, and the wisdom to know the difference" – **Serenity Prayer**

I'm starting to realize that in a lot of my dreams I was running to escape something or someone. Why was this? Fear, fear from stepping out of my comfort zone. Fear of doing something that I have never done before.

The vulture in my dream represented death, for vultures are scavengers. They feed on dead animals. Spiritually vultures symbolize purification and re-birth. This meant that I needed to kill that monster of fear and break free from my own ego.

5
Why Can't We All Get Along?

I decided to enroll into the same college that my cousin Diamond attended. I did not really hang out with her on campus because we had different class schedules. I was pretty much on my own. One day during lunch I heard a lot of noise outside of the cafeteria. I needed some fresh air, so I went to see what the fuss was about.

There were different fraternities who decided they wanted to battle in dance as the characters had done in the movie "Stomp the Yard." I enjoyed the show until the dance battles turned into fight battles.

I then went back into the cafeteria but that meant nothing. The fights continued and both groups came inside where I was. It was like a stampede.

There was a gate that I climbed so that I would not get hurt. Once they left, I went to the other side of the building. I then went down a case of stairs into another parking lot where I thought no one would be, but everyone soon made their way where I was.

I ran into a guy whose name was Ralph. Ralph was tall,

buff, and strong, with a dark-skinned complexion. He approached me and introduced himself. I asked him "Why do they have to fight all the time?" What were they trying to prove?

One guy gave me a gun to wear on my hip for protection. That is when Ralph saw two guys jumping someone and went to help. Ralph grabbed both males by the collar and slung them over a hole that was in the ground.

One of them fell in the hole and the other on the ground. Ralph then walked away but the guy who fell in the hole climbed out and ran behind Ralph. The guy beat Ralph across the head. Suddenly, one guy came beside me and tried to grab my gun out of the holster. He wanted to shoot someone who he had been wrestling with. I fought him off and went back inside.

This did not end the disaster. A big, fat, nasty looking guy approached me to try to get a hug. He claimed that I was his girlfriend. I began running until I saw Diamond with her friends.

They all came to my rescue, beating the guy on his head. He took off running and told me that it was not over. I woke up in relief.

Interpretation:

In the dream there were two groups of fraternities dancing and fighting. When organizations of such dance it symbolizes unity. Back in the day, when worshipers shifted their feet and stomped in circles, it symbolized the connection between the past present and future.

The fighting as well as the metal gun in the dream meant that I needed to stop worrying about the inner conflicts with myself and focus on the positive, energetic rhythms of my life.

Climbing the fence in the dream meant that once I had controlled my worries, I would soon be able to climb the ladder of success.

There were two instances in the dream where someone got hit in the head. To get hit in the head means that one should fight for their own beliefs. I knew at that time that I needed to get my mind right.

6
Worth A Million Smiles

What is the first thing that comes to mind when you hear that a person dreamed about fish, who is pregnant? Well in this case, things were different. I just so happened to be in a room with a lady who was holding a fish. Not only was she holding a fish, but the fish was cradled over her right shoulder. Yes, she was holding the fish over her shoulders like a baby and patting the fish.

That's not the only thing that had me tripping. The lady then laid the fish on a table because something was wrong with it. I looked at the fish and the fish looked at me with all smiles. You know I was like, "what the what"! What in the world is this?

What kind of fish has teeth? I thought it was going to start talking. The fish ended up being okay and I went about my business.

Interpretation:

I thought I was tripping. As soon as I had awakened from

my sleep, I immediately researched -- Fish with Human Teeth. I had never seen anything like this in my entire life, so I knew that this dream too had to have come from above.

During my research I found the ugliest fish with the dirtiest teeth, I had ever seen. The sheepshead fish is the fish who have these human teeth. I had to find out what a fish, living outside of water, with a mouth full of teeth symbolized.

I found out that this was a reminder that God would soon be blessing me abundantly, above all that I could think or ask. The fish symbolizes prosperity and abundance. The teeth symbolize emotions, money, transformation, and spiritual development.

Finally, dreaming of fish living outside of water means that you have some disappointment in your life, and you need to make a change. No one can tell me that my God does not have a sense of humor. This was an interesting way to send a message to me, and I was glad to have gotten the message.

7
Little Sunshine

Never underestimate your children. God will use anyone to get his message across, even the little ones. My daughter is a highly intelligent princess, and she does not forget much. She is also a dreamer.

There is not a night that goes by that I do not hear her talking in her sleep. Sometimes when she is awakened, she immediately tells me what she dreamed about.

This particular day, baby girl dreamed that she was at church. She told me that she was walking through the church looking for me but could not find me. That is when one of the deacons of the church pulled her aside and led her to the sanctuary. Baby girl noticed that everyone in the sanctuary was in their rightful places, however, something just did not seem right.

She noticed that everyone had been turned into rocks. Baby girl then walked down the aisle and to the choir stand. She described an image as a "rock man". Baby girl ignored him as she grabbed the microphone and started singing. The rock man disappeared, and everyone went back to the way they were before.

Interpretation:

COVID-19 pandemic had just gotten out of hand during the time that my daughter had this dream. Everything was in disarray and the children of God forgotten who our heavenly father is.

The message from this dream was to inform us that if we do not give God the praise, the rocks will cry out. Despite my current situation at the time, I did not need no rocks crying out in my place! One way or the other, God will get the Glory. Luke 19:39-40 speaks of this.

We must also recognize that as children of God, He takes care of us. It does not matter what is going on in the world. We must continue to give God the praise, no matter what! In doing so God will continue to provide for us. We will gain comfort, peace, understanding, protection, and so forth.

8
An Answered Prayer

February 5, 2018, I had a terrible nightmare, so I thought it was. My angel, Minister Shelia D Hayes went to live in glory with my heavenly father. I still sometimes wake up with a heavy heart, as I replay the series of events leading to her death. Needless to say, it was all in God's plan.

The day after my mother passed, I made many phone calls so that my brother and I could make the funeral arrangements. I knew that my mother did not have life insurance, however, I remembered a talk that she had with me when I was in middle school.

She told me about the benefits that she with AT&T in case anything ever happened to her. I called AT&T to report my mother's death and to collect any benefits that she should have had with the company.

My mother had been vested with AT&T, formerly known as BellSouth for many years. During the phone call with AT&T, the representative told me that my mother had life insurance. I was misinformed and that was no surprise to me. I was then transferred to Fidelity who told me that there were no death benefits available.

We proceeded with my mother's burial. It was a beautiful service, with the favor of God as well as help and support from family and friends.

Afterwards, I was terribly upset. I knew what conversation my mother and I had. I also remembered the times I saw her go online to update her information with Fidelity. She had just updated her bank information months before she passed. I prayed and cried out, "Where is my mother's money?"

The very same night, God gave me this dream. In the dream my mother was running as she held my hand in hers. She dragged me to the back yard of my grandmother's house.

Once we got to the back yard, my mother started digging a hole in the ground. From the hole she pulled out a written letter, a set of keys, and a huge stash of money. Oh, what a smile did this dream put on my face! To get the chance to see her again as I had prayed also brought joy!

Interpretation:

This dream was truly a message from God. When I awakened from the dream, I laid in bed reminiscing of the joy that I felt. I then went into deep thought as I set forth to interpret this dream.

The same set of keys that was in my dream was the exact set of keys that I had in my possession. They belonged to my mother. Right now, this set of keys has her old house key, mailbox key, and storage key on the key ring. In my mind, some money must be in one of these three places.

I then thought about the letter. In the dream I did not read the letter, but I know that the only place where my mother has a lot of papers and letters is in her storage. This is when I heard in my spirit, *"the money is in your mother's storage."*

One day, about a year ago I went down to my mother's storage to go through some of her things. Everyone who I asked to help was busy. It was later revealed to me that I had to be there alone.

I had to be careful not to throw anything away. I had not found any documents about my mother's benefits, however, as I looked through her boxes, I found multiple books and sermons that she had written. I also found other documents that told me that her death was not in vain.

This particular day I had two hours of self-therapy. I laughed, cried, and showed much gratitude to the most-high God. I learned a lot that I did not know or understand about my mother, as well as why she acted a certain way at times when she was here on earth. I also realized that a lot of the things that she had done in her life was a set up for me to follow in her footsteps and be who God has destined me to be.

My mother paved the way for me. The entire time I went through her storage, I could hear her speaking to me. She would often say, "why reinvent the wheel." In other words if you have the blueprint, do not go, and create another one. Use what you already have. You can add to it if you want.

Since that day I have taken and written down the thoughts of my mother. I started the journey of writing a book in her name, however, I was led to finish and publish this book first.

In 2013, I started this book but never finished it. I also found a lot of things from my mother's old health food store in the storage. This led me to carry on her legacy by re-opening the store, "Children's Bread Health & Wellness."

This has been the most memorable dream and message thus far. I leave with you this scripture. "But remember the Lord your God, for it is He who gives you the ability to produce wealth" -- Deuteronomy 8:18. Now that you see how I used my dreams to find my purpose, I challenge you to do the same.

Let us Practice!

Steps to Interpreting Your Dreams

Follow each step (who, what, when, and where) below to unfold each dream as you also find your purpose. Picture each dream like it is telling you a story. Imagine you are watching a movie.

Who - Write down each person who you saw in the dream.

What - Write down the things or objects that you saw in your dream. (This step should be very-detailed).

When - Write down what season you were in, the time (day/night), etc.

Where - Write down where the dream took place. The exact location.

You will then research each step, detail by detail, as it pertains to your life.

Finally, put all the details together to reveal the meaning of the dream and the message from God.

Steps to Interpreting your dreams

Who - Write down each person who you saw in the dream.

_____

_____

_____

_____

_____

_____

_____

_____

_____

_____

_____

_____

_____

_____

_____

_____

Steps to Interpreting your dreams

What - Write down the things or objects that you saw in your dream. (*This step should be very-detailed*).

_____

_____

_____

_____

_____

_____

_____

_____

_____

_____

_____

_____

_____

_____

_____

_____

Steps to Interpreting your dreams

When - Write down what season you were in, the time (day/night), etc.

Steps to Interpreting your dreams

Where - Write down where the dream took place. The exact location.

Steps to Interpreting your dreams

Research each step, detail by detail, how does it pertain to your life?

_____
_____
_____
_____
_____
_____
_____
_____
_____
_____
_____
_____
_____
_____
_____
_____

Steps to Interpreting your dreams

Steps to Interpreting your dreams

Reveal the meaning of the dream and the message from God.

_____

_____

_____

_____

_____

_____

_____

_____

_____

_____

_____

_____

_____

_____

_____

_____

_____

_____

Steps to Interpreting your dreams

www.ingramcontent.com/pod-product-compliance
Lightning Source LLC
Chambersburg PA
CBHW051713090426
42736CB00013B/2679